AF581954

A Seed from the Garden of Eve

Lawanda Banks
A Seed from the Garden of Eve: A Tree Replanted

All rights reserved
Copyright © 2025 by Lawanda Banks

No part of this publication may be reproduced, distributed, or transmitted in any form or by any means, including photocopying, recording, or other electronic or mechanical methods, without the prior written permission of the publisher, except in the case of brief quotations embodied in critical reviews and certain other noncommercial uses permitted by copyright law.

—

Published by - Spines
ISBN: 979-8-89569-795-5

A Seed from the Garden of Eve

A Tree Replanted

Lawanda Banks

This book is dedicated to the greatest gifts God has given me: my son, daughter, and husband. Thank you for being my peace amid life's storms and for the joys that await me in the morning!

Preface

Embarking on the inspiring journey of self-discovery and transformation, Peppa's story resonates with a remarkable blend of resilience, courage, and grace. In "A Seed from the Garden of Eve: A Tree Replanted," readers are invited to delve into the core of Peppa's life as she navigates the complexities of her past while embracing the uncertain future ahead. This second installment of the trilogy beautifully captures her journey to reclaim her identity while nurturing her family with love and dedication.

Peppa's evolution is nothing short of profound. As she confronts the shadows of childhood trauma and the challenges surrounding female reproductive health, she discovers the vital importance of establishing boundaries and prioritizing her own well-being. Her unwavering faith in God serves as a guiding beacon, providing her strength as she bravely navigates the often turbulent waters of motherhood and personal growth. After dedicating a decade to being a devoted stay-at-home mom, Peppa makes the courageous decision to return to university, seeking knowledge and empowerment. This pivotal choice not only reignites her passion for learning but also leads her to a fulfilling career as a district teacher, where she shapes young minds and, in turn, finds her own voice.

Driven by her enterprising spirit, Peppa begins to lay the foundation for a business that reflects her dreams and values. Through both challenges and triumphs, she is committed to creating a loving sanctuary for her children—a place where safety, support, and affection thrive. As she replants the seeds of hope and possibility in her life, Peppa beautifully illustrates that transformation is not just achievable; it's essential for true fulfilment.

Join Peppa on this heartfelt journey as she learns to nurture her aspirations while fiercely protecting those she loves. "A Seed from the Garden of Eve: A Tree Replanted" transcends mere storytelling; it stands as a powerful tribute to the enduring strength of love, faith, and the courage to start anew. May Peppa's journey inspire you to cultivate your own garden of growth, healing, and boundless possibilities.

One

"Heavenly Father, I come to you to lay my burdens at your feet. I feel weak, tired, and alone right now. I want to do what is right in Your eyes. I know that You have a plan for my life, one filled with joy, prosperity, peace, and happiness. I am weary of making mistakes in choosing the right partner to share my life with. I ask that You direct me to the man You intend for me—a man who will be my protector and provider here on Earth. Please reveal to me the person who will be the father of my children, my lifelong partner, and my friend. Let him come with roses; this will be my sign. I trust that You will fulfil the desires of my heart. God, I believe my prayer has already been answered, so I thank You, Lord... Amen."

As I lifted myself from my knees in prayer, I looked out of the dorm window and watched the snow fall from the sky. It had already been six hours, and it didn't seem like it was going to stop anytime soon. I began to reminisce about being at home, basking on Grace Bay Beach, when my roommate, Mary Ann, entered the room to ask if I was interested in going to the main campus to get something to eat.

We sometimes ate our meals together whenever we were free from our class schedules. That afternoon, a nice warm cup of Tim

Hortons hot chocolate and a bowl of warm soup was all that I was interested in eating, so I bundled up and walked with Mary Ann to the main campus building. I was grateful that Mary Ann was my roommate. What she became to me was an instant friend—somebody to whom I could talk while I was going through bouts of homesickness.

Everything was so different in Canada compared to what I was used to back home in the Turks and Caicos. In Canada, we were expected to recycle our plastic, glass, and cardboard items. Back home, everything went to the dump to be buried or burned. Even the way milk was sold at the grocery store was different. In Canada, grocers sold milk in plastic bags that fit into special pitchers rather than using plastic gallon bottles.

Additionally, Canada had large city buses for public transportation that required special tickets. While I had used large public buses when attending college in Jamaica, the buses in Canada were never overly crowded, and such a service didn't exist back home in the Turks and Caicos. Thankfully, Mary Ann helped me learn which buses to use to reach Zehrs grocery store, the Pen Centre Mall, and downtown St. Catharines.

Mary Ann and I had recently returned to campus after spending the week of Thanksgiving at her family's farm in the countryside. Being around her family made me yearn to be with mine. My conversations with my parents had started to improve since our last blow-up when I moved out of their house. My mom began checking in on me over the phone as the autumn months went by. With Christmas approaching, she wanted to make sure I would be home for the holidays.

Most of our talks revolved around her ideas for the decorations she planned to create for the yard, and it sounded like she would definitely need help to bring her vision to life. Just two weeks later, I would be flying back across the North American continent to my small island home.

Time flew by, and soon I was back in Providenciales, also known as Provo, settling in at my family home by Chalk Sound. I never tire of the breathtaking view of the turquoise water, which is simply picturesque. To make my return from Canada even more special, my Aunty Gova had cooked a giant pot of stewed conch and sent it on the plane from Grand Turk, so it would be waiting for me at home. No one made stewed conch as well as Aunty Gova, and she knew it was one of my absolute favorite meals.

As I dug into the hot bowl of stew, my mom went over the final plans for the yard decorations for the Christmas competition. I told her that her ideas would require extra help, so my sister Lou and I asked our friend Rommy-Mel to assist us. The plan involved constructing a 5-foot lighthouse with an actual revolving light at the top, along with a wooden cutout of a donkey pulling a cart filled with what looked like salt from the salt ponds in Grand Turk. Mom also wanted to create a complete Nativity scene featuring Mary, Joseph, Baby Jesus in the manger, and the Three Wise Men.

We worked tirelessly from dawn until dusk on various pieces and parts. We were grateful when Mom or Dad brought us some of Sweet T's fried chicken and fries to keep our energy up. The result was one of the most beautiful setups I had ever seen.

As people passed by to view the yard on Christmas Eve, they were invited to stop and enjoy some fried fish and conch fritters that Lou was preparing near the entrance at a makeshift food stall equipped with a coal stove and a speaker blasting holiday music. This was a delightful way for us to celebrate Christmas on the island of Provo. Besides visiting homes adorned with lights or admiring the holiday wreaths and the giant Christmas tree in the downtown area, there wasn't much else to do in Provo. Many people who had relocated to Provo from Grand Turk, Salt Cay, or South Caicos had already left the island and were celebrating mainly in Grand Turk.

That Christmas spent with my family filled my heart with joy as I could spend time with my siblings and parents. Mom and Dad seemed proud as they told their friends that I had returned home from Canada for a couple of weeks and that I was studying Child Psychology there. These simple gestures made me feel loved.

Returning to St. Catharines in the bitter cold and waist-deep snow in early January was something I was not ready to face. Day by day, it seemed to get even colder. To make matters worse, I began experiencing extremely painful periods and knew I needed to see a doctor. Fortunately, there was a clinic on campus where the doctors could start a new treatment plan that required me to receive Depo-Provera injections every three months. The hope was that these shots would reduce the frequency of my periods and lessen the pain. I would need to follow up with a specialist after the first round, with the appointment set for sometime in March.

However, this medication came with potential side effects, including bone loss or the early development of osteoporosis if used beyond two years. This made me feel pressured and worried that I might lose the chance to ever have children.

Two

My friends Leola, Naa, and Thule, whom I met on campus during the fall, all rallied around me to cheer me up when I wasn't feeling well. On the occasions when I felt well enough to socialize, we sometimes went to downtown St. Catharines for a night of dancing at the popular club in the city called L3. Once I got to the dance floor, I didn't want to leave unless I needed to use the restroom or grab a cup of Coca-Cola—or even just a cup of ice from the bar to keep me going. During this time, music from popular artists like 50 Cent and Sean Paul was hot on the music scene and kept us energized throughout the night.

One such night in February 2003, I was doing my usual thing, dancing alone on the dance floor, when a young, raunchy, and semi-aggressive man I didn't know approached me from behind and began gyrating against me. Taken aback, I turned around and said, "Get off of me; I do not want to dance with you!" In response, the stranger pulled out a wad of cash from his pocket and began waving it in my face. This act pushed me to a whole new level of upset, and I shouted angrily at him, "You don't know me! Who do you think you are?"

Out of nowhere, a young man approached us from across the floor, got between the unwelcome man and me, and whispered something in his ear. I didn't know what he was saying, so I called the bouncers and let them know what had just happened. Three bouncers accompanied me back to the dance floor, and I pointed out the disrespectful young man to them. Instantly, they snatched him by the arms and tossed him down the stairs at the back of the club.

After that was taken care of, I scanned the dance area to see if I could find the man who had intervened during the initial confrontation. When I found him, I asked if he could come downstairs because I needed to talk to him. Filled with anger, I wanted to confront him, thinking he was the other guy's friend. He quickly corrected me, explaining that he knew the man but was in no way his friend. He had whispered in the man's ear to back off if he didn't want any trouble. I thought it was admirable that this kind stranger took the time to step in and protect me, like a bonafide man should, during my moment of distress.

Relieved that Mr. Bonafide was not friends with the disrespectful young man, I felt more inclined to talk to him as I vented my frustration, using a few colourful Jamaican Patois words. He immediately noticed my accent and asked if I was Jamaican. "I'm not from Jamaica; I'm from the Turks and Caicos." Mr. Bonafide looked puzzled and inquired, "Where in the world is the Turks and Caicos?" I explained that it's a British territory, a group of islands found at the bottom of the Bahamas. He was excited to meet someone from a place he had never heard of before.

Although I was still annoyed that my fun night of dancing had been rudely interrupted, I began to say goodnight to Mr. Bonafide and was about to grab a cab back to campus. He said, "Don't let that guy ruin your night. Why don't you let me get you a drink and come upstairs to dance with me? What would you like to drink?" Looking at his kind face and trusting eyes, I agreed to hang out a bit longer with Mr. Bonafide. "Okay... I'll have a Coca-Cola, thanks." Shocked, Mr. Bonafide looked at me and asked, "Is that all you want?" After reassuring him that I prefer to have

Coca-Cola, ice cubes, or water when I dance, he obliged, and we headed back upstairs to the dance floor.

I was having a wonderful time dancing to Sean Paul's "Gimme the Light" and a few other popular hip-hop songs. After a while, I felt exhausted and told Mr. Bonafide that I was ready to go outside to catch a cab and head back to my dorm room for some rest.

"You don't have to get a cab; let me drive you to your dorm," Mr. Bonafide offered.

"I don't know... I don't know you well enough," I replied cautiously.

"I promise you that I will not harm a single hair on your head. You can trust me," Mr. Bonafide assured me, looking deeply into my eyes. Something inside me felt that I could trust him, so I accepted his offer to take me back to campus.

Then I noticed that Mr. Bonafide was not alone; three other young men were following behind us. "This is my ride here," Mr. Bonafidc said, pointing to an old model four-door car.

"Oh, okay!" I replied, preparing to walk toward the passenger door.

"No, I'm just kidding; this is actually my car over here," he said, gesturing to an SUV.

"Why did you say that the other car was yours?" I asked.

Mr. Bonafide replied, "I just wanted to see what you would say. I wanted to know if you were materialistic or not."

Laughing, I said, "How can I judge someone else's car when I don't even have one? I'm just thankful that you have a car to take me home."

Feeling proud of his vehicle, Mr. Bonafide said, "Well, this is a 2003 Chevy Trailblazer."

Looking confused, I asked, "Trailblazer? What is that? I've never heard of that kind of car before. I don't know much about name-brand cars; I'm just a young woman who enjoys simple things."

Mr. Bonafide opened the passenger door for me, and he and

his friends entered the vehicle. After a brief introduction, he said, "Peppa, these are my friends Kai, June-Bugg, and Jose." They all greeted me in unison, and I responded while playfully warning them not to put their hands on me. I fastened my seatbelt and relaxed as Mr. Bonafide tried to figure out how to get to the Brock University campus. I was no help in this situation as I am terrible with directions and was only familiar with the bus routes. I was relieved when Mr. Bonafide finally located the campus entrance.

Once we arrived at the dorms, Mr. Bonafide safely walked me to the entrance of my dorm building, holding my hand firmly to help me avoid slipping on the icy steps. We exchanged phone numbers, shared a friendly hug, said goodbye, and I walked inside, closing the door behind me.

After showering, changing into my sleepwear, and snuggling into my comfortable twin-sized upper bunk, my phone rang. It was Mr. Bonafide. He had made it back across the border and was heading home. We talked for three hours that night. I shared detailed stories about my past experiences living in the Caribbean and explained what had brought me to Canada. I also told him about my struggle with endometriosis and mentioned that I might want to have a child within the next four years. I asked if he would be interested in having children or if he would consider having a child with me. Without any hesitation, Mr. Bonafide expressed that he would be open to having a child with me.

We agreed to use the time between now and then to get to know each other better and to build our relationship. Mr. Bonafide and I made plans to meet up again the following Saturday for our first official date. In the meantime, he called me every day to check in and continue our conversations about getting to know one another.

The week passed in its usual rhythm, with me attending my various classes, hanging out with Naa, Thule, and Leolah, or spending quality time with Mary Ann. On Saturday evening, I excitedly got dressed and waited for Mr. Bonafide to come and pick me up. I still remember how he looked that day: wearing camel-coloured leather Durango boots, dark blue denim pants, a fitted sweater, and a camel-coloured leather jacket. His hair was styled in freshly done fishbone cornrows. Mr. Bonafide looked even better than he did the first night we met.

After opening the car door and helping me get comfortably seated, he played relaxing R&B music as he drove us to a fine dining restaurant in Clifton Hill, Niagara Falls. I ordered a shrimp cocktail as an appetizer and a filet mignon with mashed potatoes and steamed vegetables for my main course. When I hesitated between the lobster and the steak, Mr. Bonafide encouraged me, saying, "If you want the lobster, get the lobster." I protested, worried about the price, "But the bill is going to be too high! Look at the prices!" He reassured me, saying, "Don't worry about the price; I want you to enjoy yourself." With that, he placed our order with the waiter and provided delightful company filled with humour and comfort. I felt as if I could get used to his inviting and caring personality.

Over the following weeks, Mr. Bonafide and I spent all our free time together, from Friday to Sunday, while I dedicated Monday to Thursday to my studies or time with friends. I learned that Mr. Bonafide was a 22-year-old from Western New York, working as a welder at a nearby auto factory. He owned a vehicle and a townhouse apartment, had no children, and had just recently come out of a relationship. He treated me with care, attention, intrigue, and compassion. As each day seamlessly folded into the next, I began to feel that Mr. Bonafide was my soulmate; we complemented each other perfectly. When I struggled with bouts of sickness, he cared for me. When I felt down, triggered, or sad about my past traumas, he would hold and comfort me. Mr. Bonafide took on the role of protector and provider in our relationship.

I was introduced to both sides of Mr. Bonafide's family and became especially close with his dear great-aunt Edith and his grandmother, Big Ma. After losing my own grandmother, Tana, I found comfort in Aunt Edith and Big Ma, who helped fill the void in my life. Aunt Edith loved having us visit so she could watch us enjoy the delicious home-cooked meals she prepared: greens, stuffing, mashed potatoes, and sweet potato pies. The dishes tasted as if they were made with genuine love and affection. I found Aunt Edith's stories about life in the '40s, '50s, and '60s fascinating as she shared her experiences from times long before my own. It was impressive to learn that she was familiar with and socialized with notable figures like Frank Sinatra and Gloria Vanderbilt. Looking through photos of her youth revealed a demure and elegant woman; Aunt Edith truly was beautiful, comparable to any star on the big screen.

Shortly after meeting Mr. Bonafide's grandmother, Big Ma, she asked us, "So...when are you two going to bring me my grandbaby?" I felt relieved that she saw me as a suitable partner for her grandson. Mr. Bonafide replied that she already had grandbabies, but Big Ma insisted she wanted grandbabies specifically from him. This question became a recurring theme every time we visited Big Ma... little did any of us know that a more definitive answer would soon be forthcoming.

Three

It was a brisk weekday in mid-March when Mr. Bonafide graciously offered to drive me to my appointment with the medical specialist regarding my endometriosis. Although he had to head back to Western New York for work that evening and couldn't join me for the visit, he thoughtfully left me with cab fare to ensure I could return to my dorm hassle-free. This act of kindness truly embodied what I appreciated most about Mr. Bonafide—his unwavering support and desire to ease my financial concerns during such a challenging time.

Once at the doctor's office, I sat across from the specialist, who laid out the details of my condition. "After reviewing your medical records and the test results," he explained, "it appears that scar tissue from your endometriosis is forming around the fallopian tubes. This situation can lead to infertility, as the eggs may struggle to reach the uterus. I recommend considering conception within the next one to two years, Ms. Peppa." His words hit me like a tidal wave, filling me with urgency and anxiety. Learning I had a time frame of two years or less to conceive was overwhelming, instantly raising my stress levels.

After the consultation, I gathered the informative literature about my diagnosis and headed to the main waiting area. As I entered, I was greeted by a burst of joy from the cheerful ladies at the front desk. One of them pointed out a stunning arrangement of a dozen red roses elegantly placed in a lovely vase—an unexpected gift from Mr. Bonafide! My heart raced with delight, and a warm blush crept across my face. I was completely taken by surprise; it was such a beautiful and thoughtful gesture.

Arriving back at my dorm, I set the roses on the dining table, their vibrant colours instantly brightening the entire space. After I settled into my room, I received a call from Mr. Bonafide, eager to hear how my appointment went. I shared the prognosis, and, speaking candidly, I told him that if he wasn't ready for children yet, we could part ways amicably. Yet, staying true to his promise, he reassured me once again that he was open to starting a family with me. Overjoyed, I couldn't help but rave about the lovely roses. "How did you manage to get them to me? I thought you'd left!" I asked, genuinely curious. With a smile in his voice, Mr. Bonafide explained that he had spotted a quaint floral shop inside the doctor's office building just as he was leaving, and he arranged for the roses to be delivered to me.

The roses thrived beautifully for three wonderful weeks; they were the longest-lasting real roses I'd ever encountered. Just as I was about to toss the withered blooms, I remembered the sign I had asked God for—that the man destined for me would come with roses. Suddenly, it clicked—the flowers were not just a sweet gesture but a meaningful sign that Mr. Bonafide was indeed the right person for me. They felt like confirmation from God that he was the one He had chosen for my life.

Isn't it interesting how triggers from past experiences can surface when you least expect them? I remember visiting Western New York one day, standing in the kitchen washing dishes when Mr. Bonafide quietly approached me, expressing his affection through gentle touch. The unexpectedness of his presence and touch caused me to recoil. I felt the familiar tightening in my stomach, and a wave of electric unease rippled through me. Sensing my discomfort, Mr. Bonafide looked puzzled and gently asked what was wrong. At that moment, I opened up to him, sharing the painful memories of experiences I had endured at the ages of 10 and 14, which still lingered within me. I made it clear that I didn't believe he intended to cause harm, but the sensation of being touched without warning brought back unsettling emotions.

Acknowledging the insecurities and scars from my past was daunting, and I realized that these feelings were creeping into my blossoming relationship with Mr Bonafide. Despite these challenges, life moved swiftly during the winter semester of 2003. I kept up with my routine of attending classes throughout the week and then savouring weekends in Western New York with Mr Bonafide and his loving family. The family gatherings were truly the highlight of my visits, especially the cherished moments I spent with Big Ma and Aunt Edith. As Big Ma's health declined, I witnessed Mr. Bonafide grappling with the heartache of watching her condition worsen. His tender care for her only deepened my admiration for him, mirroring the same affection and bond I shared with my own beloved grandmother, Tana.

By the end of April, my exams were completed, and it was time for me to return home for the summer holiday. I had finished my first year of my Bachelor's program, but it was a bittersweet experience. I was glad that my classes had ended, but I dreaded being away from Mr. Bonafide for a couple of months. To cherish our time together, we visited a photo studio to take pictures that I could take home to show my family and friends—photos of the man who had become the love of my life. In just two or three short months, I was certain that Mr. Bonafide was the one for me. However, members of my family advised me to take it slowly and not rush into anything. They reminded me that, because we had been dating for such a short time, I didn't really know Mr. Bonafide yet. Understanding their concern came from a place of genuine care, I reassured my family that Mr. Bonafide had been nothing but kind, caring, and loving toward me, and I felt secure in my feelings.

In May, while at my mother's house one early afternoon, I received a phone call from Mr. Bonafide. He informed me that he had been in a car accident and was a bit bruised. I immediately wanted to catch the next flight to be by his side, but he insisted that I stay in Turks and return to Western New York after my sister Paulie's wedding, as I had been asked to participate as an usher alongside our sister Lou. Paulie's wedding took place in Miami, Florida, and many friends and family travelled from parts of the Caribbean to attend.

After the festivities, I had a conversation with one of my cousins, who shared troubling news about my younger sister that shook me to the core and plunged me back into an emotional state of anger and disgust. There was a man—a "Family Friend"—who had been a highly regarded figure in my family and a daily fixture in my grandma Tana's house. The "Family Friend" had been in our lives long before my siblings and I were born. It is one thing to get over being hurt by someone you don't know; it is quite another to cope with and deal with people who have hurt you and whom you once fondly regarded.

My cousin and I joined some of the other family members who had gathered in one of the hotel bedrooms. My cousin Brina, Aunty Babby, my sister Rokie, and my dad were present. I was deep in thought, grappling with what I had just learned about my younger sibling. I felt as if I had failed her as an older sister, thinking I should have been there to protect and comfort her. What made it even more despicable to me was the fact that my parents were still in communication with the "Family Friend."

That evening in the room, a barrage of angry words erupted from me when the name of the "Family Friend" came up during the light conversation. "Why didn't you say or do anything? How can you still speak highly of that man knowing what he did to your daughter?" The continued silence and the empty stare my dad gave me in response only fueled my anger.

"Peppa! Stop it! You are embarrassing your father here tonight!" Aunty Babby chimed in, trying to calm the situation.

"Embarrassing him? He has already embarrassed me!" I retorted. Turning my attention to Dad, I continued, "You can keep talking to those people who have harmed your children; I am done with you! I'm leaving first thing in the morning... I will see you all when I see you!"

With that, I stormed out of the room, packed my bags in my own room, and went to bed. I couldn't wait to be reunited with Mr. Bonafide and find solace in a calmer environment.

FOUR

I was thrilled when Mr. Bonafide came to pick me up from the airport in Western New York. Besides a little whiplash, he was physically alright after the very scary car accident. Seeing him face to face eased the concerns I had harboured since hearing about the accident. I was still highly emotional about everything that had transpired between my dad and me the night before in Miami. Mr. Bonafide offered comforting words and reassured me that he was there for me and that I had nothing to worry about.

While I was away in the Turks and Caicos, Big Ma's health deteriorated, and she was admitted to the hospital. After dropping off my things at Mr. Bonafide's house, we immediately visited her. Seeing her lying in bed, connected to oxygen and IVs, intensified my fear of losing her, and tears began to stream down my cheeks. I could not help but think about my grandmother, Tana, and how I had wanted to spend every moment with her while she battled her failing health in the hospital. Mr. Bonafide and I made it a point to visit Big Ma as often as we could, ensuring she had everything she needed. The summer months slipped away, and by the time fall arrived, Big Ma had passed away.

Losing Big Ma revealed another side of Mr. Bonafide. His inner child emerged, and as he broke down in tears and sobs, it was clear he was experiencing the deep pain of losing a grandmother he was very close to. Like me, he wasn't just losing a grandmother but someone he regarded as a mother. I held him close to my chest, comforting him as best as I could while my own tears silently streamed down my face.

The family arranged the funeral, we purchased the clothes that Mr. Bonafide and I would wear to the service, and Big Ma was laid to rest. October turned into November, and soon, December was upon us. I made plans to stay in Western New York to spend my first Christmas with Mr. Bonafide. It was during December that I suddenly began feeling nauseated and extremely sensitive to smells, like cigarette smoke. Normally, I wouldn't mind passing by someone smoking, but this time, my stomach felt very queasy, and I became concerned about what was happening to me. "I think I should take a pregnancy test," I told Mr. Bonafide one evening over the phone. "Wait until I come and get you tomorrow, and we can get a test from the pharmacy," he replied. While Mr. Bonafide anxiously waited on the couch, I walked upstairs toward the bathroom to take the pregnancy test.

In less than five minutes, the results were clear: two bright lines signified that I was pregnant! "Honey! Honey!" I shouted from the bathroom. "What does it say? How many lines are there?" Mr. Bonafide replied. "We are pregnant! There are two lines." Mr. Bonafide rushed upstairs, looked at the test stick, and then turned to me with a beaming smile. His eyes showed a hint of nervousness—or was it excitement? Either way, it didn't matter because I was sure my face reflected the same emotions. Mr. Bonafide pulled me into a warm embrace and promised that he would be there for me and the baby and that we were going to be our own little family.

One day, while we were at a mall in Western New York, Mr. Bonafide took me to Kay Jewelers to purchase a piece of jewellery for me. We looked at earrings, necklaces, watches, and bracelets. He then asked to see the display of wedding rings—there were so many to admire. "Which ring do you like, Peppa?" he asked. I looked at him, my face surely blushing at the unexpected question. "I like that one," I replied, pointing to a modest ring that appeared to be a timeless piece.

"That ring is too small; I want you to have a better diamond than that. What about this set?" Mr. Bonafide suggested. "Oh no, that ring is bigger than my finger! My hands are very petite; I would prefer a smaller diamond." Seeing our difference in taste, the jeweller suggested a perfect set of rings that we both liked. "I will hold these rings and give you the engagement ring when I'm ready to propose to you. I just wanted to ensure that you love the ring," Mr. Bonafide explained as we walked out of the store with the rings still in his possession. I had no issue allowing him to choose a special time to propose. He was already making my dreams come true by being the kind, caring, and loving man he was toward me.

As we lay in bed that night, all Mr. Bonafide and I could think about was how we wished his grandmothers, Eula and Big Ma, as well as my grandmother Tana, were still alive so we could share the news of our pregnancy with them. We imagined their reactions upon hearing the news. In the following days, we informed close friends and family that we were expecting our first child together. My family was thrilled that my womb was once again blessed. Reflecting on the loss of the triplets about three years prior—one at five weeks and the other two at five-and-a-half months—had planted a seed of fear within me. My family reassured me that everything would be fine and that God would help me carry this baby to full term.

Every need and craving of mine was satisfied by Mr. Bonafide, who attended every doctor's appointment with me. He was so involved with the pregnancy that he gained a few extra pounds and experienced bouts of morning sickness. I think what he had was called "sympathy pregnancy," where a man exhibits pregnancy symptoms experienced by the woman carrying his child. By the break of spring, I relocated from student housing and found a tiny two-bedroom, one-bath bungalow for rent near the Brock

University campus. It was in this snug bungalow that I prepared for the arrival of our baby. Mr. Bonafide and I shopped for all the essentials I would need upon the baby's arrival, such as clothes, toiletries, a bassinet, a car seat, a stroller, a tub, and bottles. I carefully packed tiny diapers, onesies, blankets, and other necessities in the baby bag I would take to the hospital when it was time to deliver.

Mr. Bonafide received a job transfer from Western New York to Pontiac, Michigan, during the early part of the pregnancy. This meant that instead of being less than an hour's drive away, he would now be three hours away! I was always an emotional wreck when it was time for him to leave me and return to Michigan on those dreaded Sunday afternoons. I could often be found weeping into his chest, making it a weekly spectacle in my front yard. I hated having to say goodbye to Mr. Bonafide. He would promise to return on Friday evenings, and I would watch him drive away with tear-filled eyes and a heavy heart.

Being pregnant and alone was not a pleasant feeling. I was thankful for my busy school schedule and a few friends who kept me company and helped me maintain some sanity while Mr. Bonafide was away. To me, he felt like everything, becoming the inhale to my exhale. Winter came shortly after his transfer to Michigan, and even with the threat of blizzards, heavy snow, icy roads, and bone-chilling cold, Mr. Bonafide made the three-hour trip every week to be with me. This deep demonstration of love and care only strengthened the love and trust I had for him.

Five

Spring turned into summer in 2004, and I was now sweltering from the heat while in my third trimester. The months away from home helped ease the tensions between my dad and me. It felt like yet another problem was going to be swept under the carpet, and we would move on without fully addressing the elephant in the room. Mom began reaching out to me, wanting to stay updated on my progress with the pregnancy. When she found out we were having a boy, she made it clear that she wanted to be present for the birth. She just needed to get some affairs in order first.

My sister, Jew-Jew, also expressed a desire to visit for the summer while she was off from school, which I happily welcomed. I thought it would be nice to have some extra company while Mr. Bonafide was away in Michigan for work. As soon as the semester ended, Jew-Jew made her way to me in Canada. I was thrilled to have my little sister with me. We did some light shopping for the baby, took afternoon strolls, binge-watched old movies, and marveled at how huge my stomach seemed to grow by the day. Jew-Jew helped take weekly photos to capture my gradual growth.

One Saturday morning, while Mr. Bonafide and I were snuggled in bed talking about our dreams for our little family, we envisioned having a house in the suburbs on a cul-de-sac, perfect for our future children to ride their bikes. We joked about the fact that I wanted four children while he only wanted two. Mr. Bonafide said he would go to work, cook on the grill, and cut the lawn, while I would raise and nurture the children, clean the house, and do the laundry.

At that moment, Mr. Bonafide began tapping me on the stomach repeatedly, which made me stop talking and ask what he was doing. That's when I realized he had the engagement ring on the tip of his index finger! This was his intimate and unique way of asking me to marry him, and it felt perfect. The ring sat beautifully on my hand, and I couldn't stop smiling and admiring this gorgeous token of Mr. Bonafide's love. Excitedly, I left the room to show Jew-Jew.

Mom had made plans to visit me two weeks before the baby's due date and travelled to St. Catharines to be with me for the birth, just as she promised. After gushing over the beautiful engagement ring and officially meeting Mr. Bonafide, Mom could hardly contain her joy at the fact that we were going to give her a grandson. She was shocked when she saw how much my stomach had grown. I had ballooned from 110 pounds to an impressive 145 pounds, and my stomach looked as if I had a basketball inside me. I walked with a waddle.

After showing Mom all the preparations I had made for the baby's arrival, we sat and looked at the tiny clothes one last time in the baby bag, marvelling at how adorable everything was.

"Honey, wake up... I think the baby is coming," I said, gently shaking Mr. Bonafide's shoulders.

"What? Are you sure? It's not time yet... what time is it?" he mumbled, still disoriented.

"It's almost 3 a.m... The baby is coming... I'm having a weird pain... should we wake up Mom and Jew-Jew?" I pressed for an answer. Mr. Bonafide considered waking them but ultimately decided against it. Instead, he suggested that we go to the hospital for the doctor to check me, as it might be a false alarm. Agreeing, we snuck out of the bungalow like thieves in the night and headed swiftly to the hospital, my discomfort increasing with each passing minute.

Suddenly, we saw the flashing lights of a police patrol car behind us on the dark neighbourhood street. After we pulled over, the officer approached the window, saw my condition, and offered to escort us to the hospital.

It felt like a scene straight out of a movie—where a woman in labour is rushed to the hospital by her frantic husband. "The baby's foot is coming out, and we need to perform an emergency cesarean," the doctor explained to me and Mr. Bonafide. Instantly, memories flooded my mind of the miscarriage I had suffered four years earlier during my pregnancy with the twins. The circumstances felt eerily similar, as both times, the babies were coming feet first. Fear gripped my heart, and I began to worry: would I lose this baby, too?

Feeling a gentle yet firm grip, Mr. Bonafide took hold of my hand, distracting me from my anxious thoughts. Both he and the doctor reassured me that everything was going to be all right. Thankfully, unlike the loss of the twins, I wasn't going to have to go through this experience alone; the doctor permitted Mr. Bonafide to be present for the procedure.

Sitting beside the operating table and holding my hand the entire time, Mr. Bonafide comforted me as the epidural shot was administered into my spine. Once I showed all the signs of being numb, the surgery commenced. Unable to see beyond the small curtain placed in front of my face, I focused on Mr. Bonafide, whose presence calmed me. There were moments during the procedure, as the baby was being removed when I thought I wasn't going to make it. I felt great turbulence throughout my body, and a powerful pressure began to build in my chest and head; I thought my head might explode.

Fortunately, the shaking soon stopped. Moments later, Mr. Bonafide and I welcomed our first child together—a bouncing baby boy weighing 8 pounds 5 ounces and arriving two weeks early. With yellow eyes, we could see that he was affected by a bit of jaundice, but otherwise, Nugget was perfect in every way.

As I slowly opened my eyes, I found myself in a gentle haze, caught between sleep and wakefulness in the post-operative room. Mr. Bonafide, still by my side, shared this precious moment with me, marvelling at the miracle of life that lay swaddled in the familiar hospital blanket—our son. With love and tenderness, I gazed down at the tiny being resting in my weary arms. In a moment of vulnerability, I asked Mr. Bonafide to take him, fearing I might drop this fragile new life. Overwhelmed by the morphine managing my pain, I drifted into a welcome sleep, comforted by the knowledge that our baby was safe.

When I woke up, I was greeted by the heartwarming sight of Mr. Bonafide comfortably seated in a Lazy Boy chair, tenderly feeding our little Nugget his first meal—a bottle of milk. The pure love in his gaze as he looked at our son brought a wave of emotion crashing over me. In that simple moment, I realized just how caring, loving, and protective he would be as a father. A profound sense of completeness enveloped me; I was not only a new mother but also part of a beautiful family with a partner who cherished us both.

Undergoing a cesarean section is certainly not an experience to take lightly, and the pain from the incision is something that's hard to put into words. I vividly remember the day after my surgery when the nurse removed the catheter. She encouraged me to stand, walk to my chair, and take a seat. Each movement—turning, sitting up, standing—brought waves of deep muscle pain as I feared my incision might tear. Nevertheless, with perseverance, I slowly made my way to the restroom and brushed my teeth. On the second day post-surgery, I had the daunting task of holding our precious baby and walking down the corridor and back. Admittedly, I thought the nurses may have been overly optimistic, but with a bit of encouragement and strong determination, I did it.

The day after Nugget's arrival, Mr. Bonafide had to return to work, leaving me feeling a bit lonely in the hospital, especially when visitors' hours ended. I anxiously anticipated his return four days later, just in time to bring us home. I couldn't have been more grateful for the support of Jew-Jew and my mom, who were with me during our first days at home with Nugget. Their unwavering assistance allowed me to rest and recover while they took care of our newborn. Each day was a joyous revelation as I gazed into Nugget's eyes, amazed by his presence. Sometimes, in those quiet moments, I felt as if he were a tiny parasite, instinctively latching onto me for nourishment. The reality of having him in my life felt surreal—I loved him deeply yet couldn't quite believe he was truly mine.

As the first week at home unfolded, reality began to settle in, and my body started to sync with Nugget's needs. I learned to recognize the signs of his hunger as my body prepared for our feeding times in perfect rhythm with his cries. Breastfeeding initially posed its challenges; my nipples were raw, and I often questioned if it would ever get easier. Yet, one day, the discomfort faded, and Nugget began to latch on correctly, resulting in a seamless connection between us.

Adjusting to life at home with Nugget took some time, and I cannot express enough how grateful I was for Mom and Jew-Jew's presence during this transformative period. Even with the three of us sharing the responsibilities, we often found ourselves exhausted, relying on one another for support as we nurtured Nugget and balanced daily tasks. My mom, in her infinite wisdom, was an incredible help during my recovery. Each morning, she ensured I started my day with a nutritious breakfast and a warm cup of milk. When it came time to give Nugget his first bath, she imparted her time-tested wisdom, patiently teaching me the ins and outs of baby care. Her gentle guidance reassured me, and her presence was a source of strength as I navigated my own recovery after major surgery.

Simple tasks, which I once took for granted, like getting out of bed, sitting, and reaching for a cup, suddenly required assistance. Yet, with my mom by my side, I felt supported and cherished as I embraced my new journey into motherhood. Each day brought its own set of challenges and victories, and I knew that with love, support, and a little determination, we would thrive as a family.

Having Jew-Jew's helpful hand and watchful eyes over Nugget did not go unnoticed. Jew-Jew was on baby monitoring duty whenever I needed a nap. Although I knew Nugget was in capable hands with his aunt, it was difficult for me to remain asleep in my room upon hearing his cries. I would wake up immediately and call out, "Jew-Jew! Is he okay? Why is he crying?" Jew-Jew would reassure me, shouting back from the living room, "He's crying because he's a baby! Go back to sleep!" Moments later, my door would open, and Jew-Jew would bring the baby for me to see. I would hold him, kiss him on the cheek, and then Jew-Jew would bossily order me back to sleep as she left the room with Nugget in tow. I knew I would miss Jew-Jew and her craziness when she went back home, so I allowed myself to savour every moment we had together.

Mr. Bonafide called often throughout the day, checking in on us and expressing how much he missed us. He couldn't wait to return to Canada to see us. When Mr. Bonafide finally saw Nugget, he was shocked, astonished, and amazed at how much he had grown. Mr. Bonafide marvelled at how alike he and Nugget looked as babies—it was as if Nugget was a carbon copy of him. The fatherly pride beaming from Mr. Bonafide's face quickly changed, however, when he realized that Nugget was sitting on his lap and had just had the biggest poop of his life up to that point. "Please tell me Little-Man is not taking a dump in my lap! Peppa, get your child...Jew-Jew, your nephew needs you!" We all laughed at the spectacle unfolding before us.

There was an explosion of runny stool coming out of both sides of Nugget's diaper, flowing down both legs of his pants. "Help me! Help! The doo-doo is coming out of his pants!" Mr. Bonafide exclaimed as he quickly stood up, holding the baby away from him, which startled Nugget and made him cry. Taking Nugget from Mr. Bonafide, I began to soothe him, saying, "It's alright, honey...Momma can clean you up...it's just Daddy being afraid of a little doo-doo."

Mr. Bonafide emerged from the kitchen, having just washed his hands, with a plastic grocery bag in hand. Overhearing me, he continued with his theatrics, "A little doo-doo? I have never seen a baby poop so much! Here, you can put the pants in this bag so I can throw them in the trash." Looking at him in confusion, I replied, "These pants are not going in the garbage; this is the first time he's wearing them. You can easily wash them off outside by the faucet and then place them in the laundry."

After placing the poop-filled pair of pants in the plastic bag, I handed it to Mr. Bonafide and said, "Here you go...welcome to fatherhood!" I then turned my attention back to cleaning up Nugget, laughing as I watched Mr. Bonafide halfheartedly walk outside to rinse the pants clean of the poop.

As the end of August quickly approached, it was time for Jew-Jew to return to Turks and Caicos for the upcoming school year. My mom decided to extend her trip and remain with me for a few more weeks to help me as I prepared to return to classes. By the time September arrived, I had become quite skilled at nursing Nugget and willingly offered him milk, especially when I felt full. As I started my final year of my bachelor's program, I looked forward to completing my courses and graduating. I ensured that, in addition to purchasing my school supplies, I gathered a few items to store and keep the milk fresh that I would need to express while on campus. I did not enjoy expressing milk as much as I enjoyed nursing; I appreciated that nursing allowed us to bond during our special time together, deepening the nurturing spirit within me.

As October came, I began to feel the full strain of being a new mother while managing a full course load. It was also time for my mom to return home to Turks. At this point, she suggested taking Nugget home with her until the end of the semester. I agreed as it was customary in my culture for grandparents to watch young children while their parents studied abroad. I didn't think to consult Mr. Bonafide about the decision; I nonchalantly let Nugget go with her.

When Mr. Bonafide made his regular trip from Michigan to St. Catharines and discovered that our baby was gone, he was livid. I apologized wholeheartedly, but he couldn't understand how I could send our newborn away. After I explained that it was customary in my culture, I honestly thought he wouldn't have a problem with it. However, I felt terrible when I realized I hadn't even allowed him to say goodbye to his son. Eventually, Mr. Bonafide found it in his heart to forgive me. He recognized that I, too, was suffering from my decision.

I began to question my own judgment in agreeing to send Nugget to Turks with my mom. How could I have made such a decision? My body immediately rebelled against me. My breasts became engorged with milk, and Nugget wasn't there to nurse. I felt guilty as I manually pumped my breasts, watching the milk go to waste down the kitchen sink. I imagined that Nugget must have been showing signs of separation from me as well, and I wondered how he would react during feeding time without me there.

As days turned into weeks apart, I longed to hold my baby just as much as I ached to hear his babble, sneeze, or cry. Calling my mom to check on Nugget became more painful as I listened to her tell me how much he was growing and how healthy and happy he was. I felt as if I were missing important moments that I would never get back. However, I came to realize that even in our pain, God has a purpose for everything. As much as being apart from Nugget hurt both Mr. Bonafide and me, it turned out to be a blessing in disguise. Within weeks of being away from both Nugget and Mr. Bonafide, my mental and emotional state plunged into a deep depression and sadness, a struggle only the might and healing power of God could help me overcome.

One Sunday, the evening was winding down as Mr. Bonafide

and I enjoyed a late dinner together. He was nestled comfortably on the kitchen floor, treating me to a delightful foot massage while playfully reminding me about his upcoming trip to Michigan after I left for campus. He planned to take a short nap before hitting the road, so by the time I returned from school, he wouldn't be around. In his classic light-hearted manner, he jested that since he couldn't take me along, he would be "taking my pretty toes" instead. He grabbed a butter knife from his plate and pretended to snip at my toe, both of us bursting into laughter.

After we tidied up the dishes, we shared a sweet goodnight kiss and drifted off to sleep, feeling content. The next morning, I woke up early and, as always, kissed Mr. Bonafide goodbye before heading to the bus stop. However, as I arrived at the bus stop, I noticed an unexpected wave of anxiety washing over me; my heart raced, and I struggled briefly for breath. By the time I reached campus, my mind was swirling with uneasy thoughts.

When I settled into my morning lecture, those feelings intensified into panic. Glancing anxiously at the double doors of the lecture hall, I found myself caught up in a fictitious scenario where Mr. Bonafide might burst in with a buther's knife, intent on harming me. The thought felt surreal and it triggered an urgent need to escape the classroom. I dashed down the hallway, glancing back and around, desperately seeking reassurance that Mr. Bonafide was nowhere in sight.

As I rushed through the corridor, a psychology professor noticed my distress. She approached me with concern, and I realized that I needed help. With her support, I was guided to speak with a therapist on campus. In the calm of the therapist's office, I began to articulate my fears, inadvertently mentioning a knife and my worries surrounding Mr. Bonafide. The therapist listened attentively and suggested a safe house where I could stay temporarily if necessary.

Feeling a mix of relief and fear, I was instructed to call Mr. Bonafide and explain my feelings, specifically that I needed some distance for my mental well-being. When I dialed his number, his voice came through, still thick with sleep, "Hello?". My emotions surged, and I cried, "I need you to bring my house key to me on campus... I don't feel safe with you around. I think you want to stab me to death!"

There was a pause before he responded with genuine concern and bewilderment, "Peppa, what are you talking about? Where are you?" His worry was palpable, and that made me feel both sheltered and vulnerable at the same time. I took a deep breath and replied, "I'm at school talking to a therapist... Please, can you bring me my house key? I'll be waiting at the campus entrance." I hung up, overwhelmed by emotions, yet knowing I had taken a step towards addressing my feelings head-on.

In a moment filled with deep emotions and uncertainty, Mr. Bonafide grappled with my words, feeling misunderstood. It pained him to think I could imply he would harm me in any way; after all, he had always been nothing but kind, loving, and gentle towards me. As I waited for him outside the campus entrance, the sight of his anguish when he returned my key tugged at my heart-strings. It was a poignant moment, and it made me reflect deeply on what had just transpired. I turned to my therapist and admitted, "I feel confused; I'm not thinking clearly at all. There's no way Mr. Bonafide could hurt me; I'm just missing my baby!"

When I mentioned my baby, my therapist's immediate concern shifted to the safety of my child. I reassured her that my precious three-month-old son, Nugget, was in the loving care of my mother in the Turks and Caicos, completely safe. The therapist gently explained that what I was experiencing was an indicator of postpartum depression coupled with an episode of postpartum mania. These terms were entirely new to me; my understanding had only encompassed the notion of women experiencing the "baby blues" after giving birth. She kindly offered me resources on postpartum depression and encouraged me to consult my primary care doctor about potential treatment options.

It dawned on me how swiftly I had slipped into a state of

depression. Reflecting on everything that had unfolded that day, I recognized that seeking help was not just necessary but vital. I felt apprehensive about the journey toward mental clarity and healing, fearing that I would have to navigate it alone, and I couldn't shake the worry that Mr. Bonafide might not forgive me.

As I began to calm down and my heart rate slowed, I decided to reach out to Mr. Bonafide for a conversation. Unfortunately, he wasn't in the right frame of mind and ended the call quickly. This left me feeling defeated and fearful that I had jeopardized our loving relationship.

Yet, even in our darkest moments, divine guidance often shines through. Before the night was over, Mr. Bonafide called to check on me. His genuine concern for my well-being was a comforting lifeline, and I felt an immense wave of gratitude wash over me at the sound of his caring voice. That small act of kindness helped soothe my anxieties.

Starting antidepressants was an intimidating prospect, and I was prescribed Effexor. Initially, I struggled with the side effects, which transformed my vibrant personality into one that felt overshadowed and lacking energy. My appetite vanished, and the thought of eating became unappealing. As my weight plummeted, Mr. Bonafide stepped in to support me by purchasing Ensure drinks to help maintain my nutrition.

Together, we confronted our concerns about the medication's effects and agreed to seek a different path to healing. I communicated with my doctor about my decision to stop taking the antidepressants due to their impact on my well-being.

We agreed that my first focus should be on nurturing my eating habits. Every weekend, Mr. Bonafide took me grocery shopping for healthy fruits and snacks, and I felt so grateful for his support. My friends—Naa, Thule, and Leolah—embraced me with warmth and friendship. They dedicated their time to uplifting me during their busy school schedules.

Naa would often sleep over at my house for a day or two during the week, or I would visit and stay at her place as well. I appreciated having someone to talk to before falling asleep, and my dear friend Naa was perfect for those late-night conversations that sometimes turned emotional. I have cried and expressed my gratitude to Naa many times for her thoughtful love and consideration.

As the weeks passed, my appetite improved, and I began to crave specific foods: perogies and eggs for breakfast; toasted turkey and cheese sandwiches with berries or grapes for lunch; and usually rice with chicken or spaghetti and meatballs with a salad for dinner. I particularly loved the Chow Mein noodles served at the food court in the Pen Center Mall. Sometimes, Thule would take Naa and me to the mall, and I would rush straight to the Chinese restaurant to order my favourite treat: a large order of Chow Mein. Often, Naa and Thule would hang out together at my house when we weren't on campus between classes. Thule gave the best hugs and always seemed to help me snap out of any depressive moods whenever she noticed I was drifting.

Fully sharing my thoughts and feelings helped Mr. Bonafide and my friends to understand the changes needed in my routine that could bring me back to my regular self. Leolah would take me to her home, where I spent most of my time discussing the power of God and the blessings of life with her mom, Beulah, and her dad, Lionel. I felt no shame in expressing my need to cry out and praise the Lord during our fellowship. One day while I was visiting, we prayed for the healing of my mind and the strengthening of my spirit. God answered our prayers as I felt the weight of postpartum depression begin to lift from me. He seemed to have a mighty way of keeping me safe through life's trials, placing people in my path with spiritual purposes to keep me grounded in faith and maintain my complete trust in Him. I believed that God had brought Leolah into my life during that time because He knew I would need her parents' support. I felt true love and compassion from Leolah and her family, and was thankful for the time we shared.

It became clear that I needed to start looking for childcare options for Nugget, as I would require someone to watch him while I attended classes. With no family in St. Catharines, I had to find someone I could trust. While discussing my dilemma with Leolah, she suggested her friend Natalie, who did childcare from her home during the week. I spoke with Natalie on the phone, and she assured me that she was experienced with infants. Sensing my nervousness, Natalie invited me to her home to see the environment where Nugget would be cared for. Fortunately, her house was less than a five-minute drive from mine and was well-kept to a cleanliness standard I found comfortable. With a solid plan in place for Nugget's care, my tension and anxiety levels began to decrease significantly, leaving me to focus on keeping my emotions under control.

I was filled with anticipation as December approached, eagerly counting down the days until the end of the semester. The moment it was confirmed that I would be returning to Turks, I joyfully packed my suitcase, brimming with excitement. What typically feels like a brief wait seemed to stretch on forever, each minute amplifying my eagerness. The thought of finally being reunited with my baby filled my heart with a delightful flutter and brought tears of joy mixed with a touch of anxiousness. I found myself wondering if Nugget still remembered me or if he had grown fond of someone else in my absence. As I mulled over these feelings, I made a heartfelt promise to myself: I would never let this kind of separation from my child happen again. The distance between us felt so unnatural and heavy on my heart. Deep down, I understood that having Nugget with me would nurture my maternal instincts. I was certain that once he was back in my arms, everything would fall into place. With the invaluable support from friends like Naa, Thule, Natalie, Leolah, and Beulah, I formed a small but steadfast community in St. Catharines that I could depend on to help care for my little one.

As I arrived at the airport, my dear sister Jew-Jew was eagerly waiting for me outside the arrivals area. Her radiant smile instantly lifted my spirits as we shared in the collective excitement of this long-awaited moment—seeing my child after three gruelling months. The last time I had held Nugget, he was just a tiny eight-week-old baby; now, he was five months old, and the thought of that transformation had me buzzing with anticipation. Jew-Jew kept exclaiming, "Girl, you won't believe your eyes when you see your baby!" I could hardly contain my enthusiasm as we made our way to the house; it felt as if my feet barely touched the ground.

"He's in here sleeping," Jew-Jew announced as we entered one of the bedrooms.

There was Nugget, peacefully asleep and looking absolutely perfect! It was incredible to see how much he had grown! I couldn't help but notice his chubby little arms and legs and, of course, his perfectly handsome face, radiating peace and contentment. "Oh my God! Look at my baby! Look at my baby!" I exclaimed. Upon hearing my voice, Nugget opened his eyes, and we locked gazes. At that moment, I felt a connection as if he recognized me, his mother. I scooped him into my arms, holding him tightly and whispering, "Hello Nugget, it's me... Mommy... I've missed you so much." Tears of happiness streamed down my face as I turned to Jew-Jew, witnessing her share in this beautiful outpouring of love and joy.

Life, of course, can be a whirlwind of challenges. Just as I was gearing up for my final semester in my bachelor's program, I received unsettling news from the campus office regarding my scholarship funds. It turned out that they had not yet arrived since the academic year began. I urgently needed assistance from the government of Turks and Caicos to cover my tuition, or I risked being withdrawn from the program altogether. I reached out through countless emails and phone calls, sending letters and documentation from the university to highlight the urgency of my situation.

Despite my best efforts, I soon discovered that my attempts were in vain, and the allotted time for receiving the funds had passed. It was just a week or two after my removal from the program that the funds eventually came through, but unfortunately, it was too late. I was heartbroken—what would I do now? Would I return home to Turks with Nugget? Could I possibly stay in Canada? Most importantly, would Mr. Bonafide be ready to embrace a commitment to both me and Nugget, following through on our plans to wed and build a life as a family? The thought of living with Mr. Bonafide and Nugget filled me with hope, and I could only wish that he felt the same way.

Six

After weighing our options for living arrangements,Mr. Bonafide and I decided that Nugget and I would head to Turks and Caicos for a couple of months, with plans to return to the States in April. Mr. Bonafide, seeking a change from the long, harsh winters of Michigan, was open to transferring anywhere his company he worked for operated. We explored several possibilities, including Canada, New York, and Florida, but our hearts ultimately settled on the vibrant and welcoming Dallas-Fort Worth area in Texas. We envisioned this as the perfect place to lay down roots and build our family together, with plans to marry once Nugget and I arrived and were settled in.

The Dallas-Fort Worth area was indeed an ideal location—equidistant from Western New York and the Turks and Caicos —offering the right mix of excitement and tranquility. Both of us were yearning for a fresh start, away from the influence of our families, as we wanted to create a nurturing and loving environment for Nugget. While in Turks, I secured a part-time position at the lovely Palms Resort in Provo. I was incredibly grateful to have my mom, Jew-Jew, as well as Cass and P.J., pitch in to look after Nugget as often as they could. Throughout this transition, I felt a strong longing for the moment when Nugget and I could be reunited with Mr. Bonafide, whose deep love and support made the distance hard to bear.

At the end of March, Mr. Bonafide found us a wonderful home in the DFW area, and just a few weeks later, in late April, Nugget and I made our move to Texas to join him. I eagerly embraced my new role as a stay-at-home mom and quickly established a delightful routine for Nugget and myself. Our days were filled with joyful walks to the park, shared meals, and, of course, chores. Yet, amidst all this excitement, I realized there was one important detail we needed to address: I wasn't married yet! Within just three weeks of our relocation, I was determined to set our wedding plans into motion.

I reached out to the Green Oaks Wedding Chapel and reserved a Thursday for our ceremony—the most budget-friendly option. Choosing the economical package allowed me to secure the bride and groom's dressing room, the chapel, a pastor to officiate, and a photographer. The next step was finding the perfect wedding dress, and I happily took Nugget along. At David's Bridal, I found a stunning gown priced at just $99, which fit perfectly within our budget. In total, the entire wedding, including all incidentals, came to around $1,000. Thanks to the generosity of my family, we were able to cover most of the expenses: my brother P.J. generously contributed to my dress, my sister Rokie covered the chapel and pastor, and Lou took care of the photography.

With the bulk of the costs covered, I eagerly anticipated Mr. Bonafide's return from work that evening to unveil my plans. As he set his work bag down by the front door, I playfully asked, "Do you love me?" He looked at me, a hint of confusion in his eyes, and assured me, "Of course I do... Why?" I then asked, "Do you still want to marry me?" With a spark of curiosity, he replied, "Yes... I do want to marry you." My heart soared with joy, and I exclaimed, "Fantastic! We're getting married next Thursday at 10 a.m.! It's all paid for; the only thing you need to take care of is renting your tuxedo and shoes. My family has helped make this happen, and all you need to do is show up."

A mix of surprise and delight crossed Mr. Bonafide's face as he laughed, "You don't waste any time making decisions, do you?" I smiled back and replied, "I have no time to waste! Since I'm on a visitor's visa that's only valid for two more months, we need to move quickly." Understanding the urgency of our situation, Mr. Bonafide embraced the idea of becoming a married man soon. We both recognized the importance of tying the knot—in addition to sharing our lives together, it would allow me to access medical care through his health benefits, which was essential for us. And with that, we knew we were on the right path to building our future together.

When we exchanged our marital vows, we committed to love, honour, and cherish each other, promising to support one another through both the ups and downs—whether in wealth or want, in sickness or health. Our wedding was a truly heart-warming occasion, shared with our dear friend Jermel and our son, Nugget. A heartfelt surprise awaited me the night before the ceremony when my mom arrived, saying, "There's no way I was going to miss seeing you get married!" Her gesture of walking me down the aisle and entrusting my hand to Mr. Bonafide made the day even more special. After the ceremony, we celebrated with a delightful dinner at Red Lobster, marking the joyful beginning of our journey as husband and wife.

Becoming officially married brought me a sense of relief and opened doors of opportunity as I prepared for our future together. The security of our commitment reassured me that Mr. Bonafide would honour his promises to love and support not just me but our son Nugget and any future children we may have.

As I fully embraced my roles as a wife and mother, I found immense fulfillment in caring for our home and family, delighting in the management of our household while Mr. Bonafide diligently worked to provide for us. Adjusting to life as a family of three came with its challenges, especially as we navigated the expenses that come with a newborn and my immigration process. During those initial months, my mom was incredibly supportive, lending us a helping hand financially when needed. However, I eventually knew it was time to stand on our own two feet and graciously declined her offerings. This was a pivotal moment that strengthened our resolve. While it wasn't easy to turn down Mom's generosity, I was genuinely grateful for that choice. It was important for Mr. Bonafide and I to demonstrate our ability to support ourselves and meet our needs. By tightening our financial belts and making deliberate sacrifices, we focused on what truly mattered. We cut back on non-essential spending, like dining out and shopping, and soon began to witness our savings blossom.

Seven

Shortly after Nugget celebrated his first birthday, I had a heartfelt conversation with Mr. Bonafide about trying to conceive a second child. I reasoned that it would be a wondeful opportunity if both children grew up close in age together. After engaging in thoughtful consultations with our doctors, we were thrilled to receive the go-ahead to conceive. Remarkably, just one month after I stopped taking birth control, I discovered I was pregnant!

Given my past struggle with postpartum depression after Nugget's birth, my OBGYN recommended that I take antidepressants during this pregnancy. I was prescribed Wellbutrin and Celexa with the assurance that these medications would be safe for the baby. I felt relieved knowing that I could focus on maintaining my mental well-being while nurturing our growing family.

As the pregnancy progressed, I encountered morning sickness that was more intense than what I experienced with Nugget. In light of this, Mr. Bonafide and I made the decision to enroll Nugget in daycare so I could take the time I needed to rest. Unfortunately, within just a month, Nugget came down with pneumonia. I immediately told Mr. Bonafide that Nugget would be staying home with me from then on—I was ready to take on that challenge. Caring for Nugget during his illness demanded every ounce of emotional strength I had. He had a high fever and dealt with severe diarrhoea, which was tough on his delicate skin. I diligently applied Desitin and Dr. Smith's diaper rash creams to soothe him, gently cleaning him and ensuring that he was comfortable. I can't express the immense relief I felt when Nugget finally recovered, as it lifted a weight of countless hours of nursing him back to health off my shoulders.

By November 2006, I was filled with anticipation as we prepared to welcome our second child. My doctor advised a cesarean section due to some lingering tenderness from my previous surgery with Nugget two years prior. Drawing from that challenging experience, I confidently expressed my decision to have my tubes tied during the procedure—my mantra became "two and through, thank you very much." Having this clarity allowed me to mentally prepare for the surgery and to look forward to returning home with our new addition. I even made a special request for the surgery to be scheduled after Thanksgiving, as I wasn't about to miss out on our cherished holiday feast.

To ensure everything went smoothly, Mr. Bonafide took time off from work to care for Nugget while I was in the hospital and to help me settle back at home after the baby's arrival. We transformed our living room into a cozy sanctuary reminiscent of a bear's den, filled with a large sofa, a bassinet, plenty of pillows, blankets, and the enchanting glow of our Christmas tree lights. Decorating for the holidays is a tradition close to my heart, and that year was no different. We infused our home with warmth and joy, the perfect backdrop for the final moments before my surgery and the lengthy recovery process that lay ahead.

My mom had a genuine desire to come to Texas and lend her support during this pivotal time, but I confidently reassured her that Mr. Bonafide and I had a well-thought-out plan in place. After benefiting from my mom's guidance with Nugget, I felt prepared to care for our new little one. The weeks seemed to fly by, and before I knew it, I found myself in the hospital maternity ward, lying on the operating table, ready to face the challenging procedure that would welcome my baby into the world. I was determined to be brave—for the sake of my baby, for Nugget, for Mr. Bonafide, and for myself.

Throughout the entire process, Mr. Bonafide held my hand firmly, providing calm reassurance amidst the chaos of emotions I was experiencing. Despite the overwhelming sensations in my body, the tightening pressure in my head and chest left me feeling fearful. In those moments, I found strength in my cries: "Help me, God! Help me, God! Honey... I cannot breathe... my chest! Help me, God!" But Mr. Bonafide's soothing voice cut through my cries like a gentle beacon of hope. "You'll be alright, Honey... it's almost over... you are doing great... just breathe in and out... breathe in... breathe out." Focusing on his steady breathing, I found the calm I needed to navigate that incredible moment.

Then came the moment I had been longing for—the powerful cry of my baby! It was a beautiful sound announcing the arrival of our precious baby girl, weighing in at 8 pounds and 10 ounces. Mr. Bonafide was asked to cut the umbilical cord, and it filled my heart with joy to see him so involved in this extraordinary experience.

When my sweet baby girl was finally placed in my arms, I was overwhelmed with gratitude and love. Even if it was just a fleeting moment, I was in awe of her perfection. Tams, my infant daughter, felt like the final piece of my life's puzzle. Now, I found myself complete with a loving husband, a wonderful son, and a charming daughter. Mr. Bonafide and I had created our own little family unit, and I wholeheartedly vowed to protect and cherish this new chapter. My mission was clear: to ensure my children grew up surrounded by love and safety, keeping a vigilant watch over them until they could stand on their own.

During the same time I was pregnant with Tams, I was grappling with the news of my Aunt Babby's serious illness. With my own health issues tied to the pregnancy and the doctors advising against travel, it broke my heart to know she was in the hospital in Florida and that I couldn't be with her. Thankfully, we managed to stay connected through phone calls. I reached out to Aunt Babby every chance I got, eager to hear about her condition. Despite numerous tests, the diagnosis remained elusive, and I often found myself speculating—could it be lupus or cancer? All I knew was that the medical procedures were taking a toll on her.

"I am so tired, Peppa. My body is exhausted from being poked and prodded," Aunt Babby would tell me, her voice strained yet familiar. Those words felt heavy, especially as my mom and Aunt Babby's children often encouraged her to keep fighting. But when I heard her heartache, I truly understood the deep exhaustion her illness had caused. To lift her spirits, I decided to talk about something she loved—teaching me the art of cooking a perfect pot of grits.

Cooking brought me joy, and Mr. Bonafide was always excited for a hearty meal of grits, eggs, and turkey bacon. However, I struggled with making grits. They either took too long to soften or ended up too gritty. Aunt Babby, alongside Tana and in fierce culinary competition with my other aunt, Aunty Gova, had all the expertise. Sensing her mood lightening, she graciously shared her wisdom, "To make a great pot of grits, make sure your pre-salted water is boiling rapidly before you add the pre-washed grits. Once you do, give it a good stir, cover it with a lid, and reduce the heat to low. Let them simmer for about ten minutes, stirring occasionally. Oh, and if you like cheese or butter, go for it!" It suddenly clicked—I had been missing crucial steps! I realized I hadn't waited for the water to boil properly or rinsed the grits to clear out any stubborn husks.

With this knowledge, I felt empowered, knowing I could not only improve my cooking but also brighten Aunt Babby's day with cherished memories of food and family. Our bond felt stronger than ever as we navigated these trials together.

It brought me immense joy to cook my first pot of grits perfectly, feeling Aunty Babby's pride as she shared her cherished recipe with me. Although this became one of the last lessons I received from her, I hold it close to my heart. Aunty Babby was a remarkable woman who truly appreciated the beauty in life's simple moments. Her unconditional love and radiant smile had the power to brighten anyone's day. While I missed her dearly, I found comfort in knowing that heaven welcomed a true angel when she joined the divine. Her spirit continues to inspire me, and I feel grateful for every shared memory and lesson.

EIGHT

Life in the Texas suburbs turned out to be quite different from what I had envisioned. Coming from the islands and having never lived in America before, I had formed my understanding of American culture largely through television. I dreamed of a life for my children that mirrored the joyful camaraderie of shows like "The Brady Bunch"—where there was always a bustling neighbourhood filled with children, and backyard gatherings were abundant. However, what I encountered were quiet streets and limited interaction. The rare cars passing through seemed to vanish behind closed garage doors.

Realizing the importance of social connection for my children, I took it upon myself to create a nurturing environment. I started engaging with other mothers during our late afternoon strolls or at local parks, allowing for special moments for our children to connect. Gradually, I formed valuable friendships with moms who had kids close in age to Nugget and Tams. Together, we organized playdates, visited each other's homes, and celebrated birthdays. This little community provided the social fabric I had hoped for, reassuring me about my children's social experiences. Friends like Amy, Dana, and Blair became integral parts of our lives during my decade as a stay-at-home mom.

For Mr. Bonafide and me, this journey was a new and eye-opening experience, particularly because we did not have the luxury of family support nearby. In our own childhoods, large families meant there was always someone to talk to or connect with. Now, our children, Nugget and Tams, were navigating a different landscape, with just their parents and each other as constant companions. To bridge that gap, I endeavoured to create engaging and enriching experiences for them every day.

I took on the role of their first teacher, focusing on essential early childhood skills like reading, writing, and basic arithmetic until they were ready for kindergarten. I taught them the importance of self-care, like using the restroom and tidying up after playtime. Establishing a daily schedule was crucial; it provided structure for both the children and me. I carefully planned our day to include time for breakfast, learning, cleaning, cooking, napping, playing, bathing, and bedtime. This routine not only facilitated a comforting rhythm for the kids but also alleviated my own feelings of burnout during those busy days.

Though I was determined to create stability and normalcy for my family in Texas, I was also grappling with the effects of postpartum depression after Tams was born. After being on antidepressants for over three years, I began to experience concerning side effects, including vivid hallucinations during the night. It was not uncommon for me to awaken Mr. Bonafide in the early hours, waking up in a panic, convinced that there were swarms of bees invading our space. "Honey, there are so many bees!" I would exclaim, stirring him from his sleep. Confused, he would reply, “Bees? What bees? There’s nothing there—go back to sleep.” Other times, I would perplex him by insisting that a bug had landed on the bed, prompting frantic requests for him to turn on the light. Each time, he patiently reassured me, gently revealing that nothing was there.

One night, I experienced a particularly intense episode of hallucinations that led me to believe there was a massive spider web in the corner of my room, with a giant spider sitting right in the centre. At that time, Mr. Bonafide was at work, so I decided to wake my son, Nugget, who was only six years old. "Nugget... Nugget...Wake up! There's a huge spider in my room!" I said, my voice thick with urgency. Rubbing his sleepy eyes, Nugget groggily mumbled, "What?" Unphased, I gently shook him and repeated, "There's a giant spider in my room. Please get the broom so we can take care of it."

Nugget, still half-asleep, retrieved the broom from the kitchen while I stood at the top of the staircase, anxiously waiting for him. As soon as he handed it to me, I stepped back into my bedroom and swatted at the "spider" with the broomstick with an exaggerated show of bravery. Nugget, looking perplexed by the whole scene, asked, "Mom, I don't see a spider. Where is it?" At that moment, I glanced from Nugget's tired and confused expression back to the corner where the spider had "been," and was suddenly no longer there. I realized that it was a figment of my imagination. Feeling a rush of clarity, I reassured Nugget that it must have been a bad dream. I tucked him back under his covers, feeling grateful for his understanding, and then I stepped into my room to call Mr. Bonafide. I couldn't help but feel a wave of guilt for putting my son through that. It was a humbling moment, and I realized it was time to reassess my medication. Thankfully, Mr. Bonafide was right there, ready to support me as he had before. Together, we decided to adopt a healthier lifestyle that included trips to the gym, walks in nature, meditation, and heartfelt prayers for my mental healing and clarity.

During this journey toward normalcy, I truly cherished the regular visits from my family members. My brother P.J., my sisters Jew-Jew and Cass, and my mom would make their way to the DFW area, which made for wonderful family reunions. I often thought it was more convenient for them to come to Texas than for a few of us to travel to Turks. Plus, my mom and siblings could take advantage of these visits to shop for items that were either hard to find or too expensive back home. This arrangement benefited everyone, allowing my children to bond with some of the most cherished people in my life.

I have a fond memory of when Jew-Jew visited with her two-year-old son, Tero. One day, I had stepped out for a quick errand, leaving Jew-Jew at home with my kids. When I returned, I could see that she was quite upset. “That little girl is too rude!” Jew-Jew exclaimed as I walked in. “What happened with Tams?” I inquired, sensing the irritation in her voice. Jew-Jew explained, “I went into the living room where Tams was watching 'Bubble Guppies,' and I told her I was tired of watching it, and she told me to close my eyes then!” I couldn’t help but chuckle at the situation and reassure Jew-Jew that in our home, we always let someone finish their show before switching to something else. “Why are you so upset about a four-year-old, though?” I asked, genuinely curious. Still irritated Jew-Jew replied, “That little girl has been here before! You really need the patience of a saint to deal with her, because if she was back at home, she’d be getting quite the discipline!” With a grin, I continued, “That’s why she’s with me and her father here in Texas—no one’s going to punish her for speaking her mind!” I cherished Tams’ strong will and independent spirit; it was one of the qualities that made her unique. It felt wonderful to know that she wouldn’t be a pushover in this world, and even in moments of chaos, I felt blessed to have such amazing children, each with their own vibrant and blossoming personalities.

Life with the kids was settling into a sweet routine, but I started to notice a gap in my own happiness. While I loved caring for our home and children, I realized I craved more engagement outside of those responsibilities. It struck me that Mr. Bonafide and I hadn’t been on a date in ages, and I found myself feeling isolated. With Mr. Bonafide working long hours to support our family, it started to seem to me as if he was enjoying a richer quality of life than I was. Hearing him laugh with coworkers while we chatted briefly on the phone, or knowing he was off to the gym to play basketball with friends, or the fact that he sometimes got to go and unwind at a sports bar brought a pang of envy. Even if it his outings were just a few times each month, felt like a luxury I did not have.

When I tried to express this to Mr. Bonafide, he genuinely couldn't understand how I felt. He would say, "Do you think I want to be in a noisy factory all these hours, day in and day out? I would gladly switch places and stay at home with the kids." His words were sincere, but I felt he wasn't grasping the deeper emotional isolation I was experiencing. It wasn't a lack of appreciation for the privilege of being home with our children; it was more about feeling disconnected and lonely. Thankfully, my feelings must have struck a chord with him, as he soon arranged for a professional babysitting service to step in. This opened up a wonderful opportunity for us to enjoy more date nights and social outings, allowing us to reconnect as a couple.

The situation greatly improved when our children were old enough to attend Kid's Park, a fantastic hourly childcare option at the Arlington Highlands Shopping Center in the DFW area. Kid's Park truly became our saving grace, offering flexibility with hours that fit perfectly into our lives. I relished the moments when Mr. Bonafide and I could indulge in activities we both loved —like brunches, movies, comedy shows, dancing, and karaoke. With the babysitter and Kid's Park in the mix, I felt a wave of relief knowing that Nugget and Tams were safe and happy while we rediscovered our bond.

Of course, life is full of ups and downs. Just as things were finding their rhythm, I encountered additional health challenges that began to affect me. I started experiencing heavy periods that lasted up to fifteen days, followed by days of rust-coloured discharge. This had a significant impact on our intimacy, and it was disheartening to feel like our frequency dwindled to just once or twice per month. This shift left me feeling deeply insecure. As I navigated my feelings, I often found myself grappling with thoughts that cast a shadow of doubt over my relationship with

Mr. Bonafide. The fear that another woman might capture his attention and meet his needs in ways I couldn't left me feeling vulnerable. This emotional turmoil led to moments of anxiety, sparking arguments that strained our connection. Even though he consistently reassured me of his commitment, I sometimes questioned whether his words reflected genuine feelings, or were merely intended to comfort me. However, through it all, Mr. Bonafide remained steadfastly dedicated to me and our family. His patience and willingness to engage in meaningful conversations with me were a true testament to his love. He took the time to check in regularly while at work, demonstrating his desire for open communication and mutual support. Together, we endeavoured to address my worries, fostering a safe space where I could share my thoughts without hesitation. His understanding of my fears became a strong foundation for our bond, reminding me that he was unwaveringly present, no matter the challenges we faced.

By the time I reached 29, my journey with endometriosis had come to a pivotal point, albeit not in the way we had hoped. Mr. Bonafide, my OBGYN, and I had embarked on a path involving two surgical procedures: an endometrial cryoablation and an endometrial ablation. We held onto optimism that these interventions would alleviate my heavy monthly cycles. Unfortunately, my body had its own timeline, and I continued to experience breakthrough bleeding. Ultimately, my doctor suggested that a partial hysterectomy would be the best option for my well-being. The procedure, performed laparoscopically with laser technology, was a significant step forward.

While this surgery effectively eliminated my heavy periods, it brought with it a new challenge: bladder inflammation. At times, it felt like I had merely swapped one issue for another, prompting me to lean into my faith and pray for complete healing. However, I chose to focus on the positives—the bladder inflammation was infrequent, and there were effective medications available to support me. With increased comfort and the ability to enjoy intimacy with my husband more regularly, I began to see improvements in my overall health.

Despite the progress, I remained aware of the insecurity that lingered in my heart. While I felt comfortable discussing everything with Mr. Bonafide, I recognized the value of seeking professional guidance to foster my self-esteem. Through therapy, I found a supportive space where I could delve into deeper emotional topics. It was eye-opening to uncover how my insecurities had their roots in past relationships and experiences. This journey helped me pinpoint specific aspects of myself that I wished to change, nurture, and strengthen.

Reflecting on my life, I realized that I had already overcome numerous challenges. This newfound awareness fueled my desire to emphasize my strengths and passions. I began to set both long-term and short-term personal goals, embracing a more positive outlook on life. In prayer, I sought divine assistance in releasing the burdens of insecurity that weighed heavily on my heart and mind. Simultaneously, I ventured into meditation, took leisurely walks in the park, and immersed myself in gardening and grounding myself in nature. Each day, I recited the mantra, "You are safe, you are loved, you are blessed," gradually emerging from the shadows of doubt and insecurity that had threatened my happiness. With a sincere commitment to my personal growth and a support system that uplifted me, I embraced a more confident and fulfilled version of myself, ready to face whatever challenges lay ahead with optimism and strength.

Nine

I committed to my long-term goal of being a stay-at-home mom for ten years. As I approached the final three years of that period, I began making plans for my transition back into the workforce. Having previously worked as a certified teacher in the Turks and Caicos and possessing a strong passion for teaching, I sought clarity on becoming a certified teacher in Texas. Through research on the Texas Education Agency's website, I discovered the following requirements:

1. Obtain a bachelor's degree from an accredited college or university.

2. Complete a Texas Education Agency (TEA)-approved educator preparation program.

3. Pass the required certification exams, including the Pedagogy and Professional Responsibilities (PPR) exam and all related content exams.

4. Apply for a teaching certificate or license through the TEA website after meeting all requirements.

I realized that I would have to return to school to earn my bachelor's degree. With the University of Texas at Arlington just a ten-minute drive from my home, I decided it was the right choice for me. I brought my transcripts to a meeting with an undergraduate advisor, who guided me in enrolling in the Bachelor of Science degree program in University Studies. Fortunately, several credits from my teaching diploma from Mico Teachers College and my psychology program at Brock University were transferable, which would reduce the time needed to complete the degree. The advisor also informed me about the option of obtaining my teaching certification by enrolling in UT Arlington's Master of Education Program with Initial Teaching Certification after earning my Bachelor of Science degree. With three years remaining on my ten-year goal, I chose to attend part-time, allowing me enough time to care for myself and my family.

With a clear pathway for becoming a certified teacher, my next challenge was figuring out how to afford my classes. My advisor informed me about financial aid opportunities, and I was able to meet with someone from the Financial Aid Office on the same day. During that meeting, I learned that since I was married to Mr. Bonafide, I would need access to his income tax information to be considered for financial aid, as I did not have substantial work experience in the United States and was currently unemployed.

Excited by the information I gathered at UTA, I went home and shared my plans with Mr. Bonafide. He fully supported my plans and encouraged me to apply to UTA, celebrating with me when I received my acceptance. He also helped me secure a federal student loan to cover my courses and Tams' part-time daycare expenses. Since Nugget was already enrolled in public school, that tuition would not be an additional financial burden, for which I was very grateful.

My time at UT Arlington offered me wonderful learning experiences, and I approached each course with complete focus and effort. Since I was already trained to teach remedial reading and social studies, I aimed to excel in each class, particularly in preparation for teaching those subjects to my future students. I had excellent professors who were knowledgeable in their fields; however, I found myself forming closer connections with the professors in the undergraduate History Department, such as Dr. Pinkney, Dr. Narrett, and Dr. Dulaney. Their strong passion for their subjects significantly increased my interest in the histories of the United States, Texas, and African Americans. I approached Dr. Dulaney, who was not only the African American Studies professor but was also, at the time, Chair of the History Department. One afternoon, while I was on campus, I mustered up the courage to speak with Dr. Dulaney, and I asked him if there were any employment opportunities that I could take advantage of within the department. I was thrilled when he offered me the opportunity to be his intern and help him develop a curriculum that could be used for middle and high school students on the American Civil Rights Movement. This assignment opened my eyes to the deep injustice and mistreatment of African Americans and people of colour in the United States. Having only learned Caribbean and British history, I did not know very much detail about American or African American history.

The research began with the murder of Emmett Till. After learning the details, I entered Dr. Dulaney's office with tear-filled eyes and asked him, "Was it your desire to make me cry?" His reply was, "I would have been concerned if you were not moved or affected by what you learned about Emmett. I realized that I would have to strengthen my mind and heart if I were going to take on the role and complete the task that was assigned to me. I worked for months on the project, delving deeper and deeper into the information on the movement, from Emmett Till to affirmative action. At the end of it all, I was able to produce summaries, lesson plans, a glossary of terms, and in-class activities that both Dr. Dulaney and I were proud of.

The time flew by while I was enrolled in the undergraduate program, during which I applied myself to countless hours of study in various subjects related to the social sciences. I organized study groups with classmates and took advantage of any extra credit assignments that were offered, just as a means of ensuring that I would achieve the best scores possible. I felt that if I was going to be expected to teach the content in the classroom, it was especially important to me that I was fully knowledgeable in the area.

The moment I'd been eagerly anticipating had finally arrived—I graduated with my Bachelor of Science in University Studies! It was an incredibly special day, made even more meaningful by the presence of my wonderful family and friends. My mom, dad, and my childhood friend A.G. travelled all the way to Texas to support me during the ceremony. I was also delighted to celebrate with my amazing friends: Mr. Bonafide, Nugget, Tams, Blair with her son Alex, and Kelly with her husband, Reggie. Seeing everyone there filled my heart with immense joy, knowing they were there to witness this personal milestone.

With my bachelor's degree in hand, I took a major step closer to fulfilling my dream of becoming a teacher in Texas. However, my journey didn't end there—I now needed to complete one more year in the Master of Education program to earn my initial teaching certification. I happily enrolled again at UTA, excited to dive into this next chapter. It was during this time that I had the privilege of learning under the remarkable Dr. Diane Galloway. Our evening classes, filled with just about ten students, created a nurturing environment where we could thrive. Dr. Galloway encouraged us to develop the necessary skills in curriculum and instruction to truly excel in our teaching careers.

I was incredibly grateful to Mr. Bonafide for his unwavering support throughout my educational journey. He kindly adjusted his work schedule to days, ensuring he could care for Nugget and Tams in the evenings while I attended class. His understanding made a world of difference in helping me reach my goals. Though he voiced some concern about my study hours and how it was affecting my health, I was fueled by my determination to earn the best possible scores.

I couldn't contain my excitement when I successfully completed my student teaching, fulfilled my practical hours, and passed the state exam! Proud that I was now certified to teach

Middle School Language Arts and Social Studies, I was filled with optimism and enthusiasm for the bright future ahead of me!

Around the same time I acquired my Texas Teacher Certification, I was granted my United States citizenship. Mom travelled to Texas to attend the ceremony. With all the things needed for me to comfortably work in the country, I set my sights on employment opportunities and attended multiple interviews and district-wide job fairs in Arlington, Mansfield, and Fort Worth. Just when I thought that nothing was going to be offered to me, I was granted employment with the Fort Worth Independent School District (ISD) as a middle school, 7th-grade Texas History teacher.

Working in Fort Worth came with the usual challenges faced by many educators who have worked in an inner-city school. With crowded classrooms, few resources, and a surrounding community facing economic difficulties, I quickly learned that there was only so much I could do as an individual teacher to uplift the minds and perspectives of the students. There were those cases that were far beyond my sphere of influence, yet there was a certain amount of resilience that could be seen among many of the students who attended the middle school. Regardless of the negative factors that plagued the school and the surrounding community, I came across a majority of the students who wanted to learn and apply themselves to the academic demands, despite their daily struggles. I also developed a great level of respect and admiration for many of my colleagues who worked passionately and tirelessly to reach their students in whichever way they could.

One of the problems that I noticed immediately as a seventh-grade Social Studies teacher was that there were several students in each of my five groups of classes I taught who were reading well below their grade level. Yet, these students were expected to participate in class by reading the grade-level text and content that surpassed their understanding. I tried, as best I could, to create lesson plans that allowed for oral discussions, video imagery, and art to help deepen their understanding. Additionally, I offered after-school classes for a few students who desired to improve their grades in my class.

I quickly learned within a few weeks of working at the middle school that some students lived in homes without water, electricity, or even food. To help address their needs, I began to furnish my classroom with snacks like granola bars and crackers, as well as personal care items such as deodorant, dental supplies, and sanitary napkins. Despite my efforts to stretch my salary by providing these items, it was still not enough to truly alleviate my students' struggles. Each day, at a certain time, I would hop into my car and drive out of the inner city, returning to my suburban home while many of my students faced the harsh realities of waiting for them at home. I realized that all I could do was try my best, which meant nurturing meaningful relationships with my students.

The guidance and support I received from the administration, particularly from the principal, Mrs. Woods, bolstered me during my challenging moments as a new teacher. One significant moment of kindness was shown to me by Mrs. Woods, who advised me that while having a job was crucial, it was equally important to make time for family. My world was shaken early one morning when I received the devastating news that Martin, the father of my nieces, Nya and Abi, had tragically died at the hands of a drunk driver while returning home from fishing. Martin was a gentle, loving, jovial, and kind soul. Being the same age as my brother P.J., I viewed Martin not only as my niece's father but also as a brother. The impact of Martin's death hit me hard, and I cried uncontrollably. I desperately wanted to be home to support my sister, Lou, and the girls. After purchasing a ticket, I travelled home for the weekend to be present for Martin's funeral.

Martin's death reinforced how fragile life can be and how quickly circumstances can change. I felt immense pain for my sister Lou, who had to find the strength to tell her young daughters that their father was gone. This loss made me cling even closer to Mr. Bonafide as I began to fear losing him too. I experienced sleepless nights filled with uncontrollable sobs over the loss of Martin, and from nightmares of losing Mr. Bonafide. Martin was indeed a very special person whose life had been taken far too soon.

During this time, my home life also changed significantly as both Nugget and Tams started attending elementary school. I had to rely heavily on Mr. Bonafide to take on additional responsibilities due to my work schedule. He agreed to continue working the night shift from 10 pm to 6 am, which allowed him to help in the mornings by making breakfast, packing lunches, and seeing the kids off to school. Afterwards, he would sleep until around 3 pm, ready to welcome the children home. Mr. Bonafide also took on most of the dinner preparations during the week. In return, I happily prepared breakfasts and dinners for our family on the weekends. I used Friday evenings, Saturdays, and Sundays for household chores and to spend quality time with Mr. Bonafide and the children. I also managed to go to the gym to work out with Mr. Bonafide, typically on the weekends, as my responsibilities as a full-time teacher kept me busy throughout the week.

One Saturday afternoon, Nugget came to me in the living room while I was listening to music and folding laundry. I could see something was wrong because he was trying to fight back tears. I turned down my music and asked, "What is the matter? Why do you look so upset?" Hearing the concern in my voice, Nugget took a deep breath and replied, "There is this guy in the game who keeps saying mean things to me. It feels like he's trying to bully me, and I don't like it." I responded to my son, "Nugget, those people in the game cannot harm you; they don't know who you are or where you live. They are not your real friends anyway. If anyone online says anything that makes you feel uncomfortable, you can simply block them." Nugget's expression suggested he had completely overlooked this fact or had not even considered using the block or unfriend option.

Within the next fifteen minutes, I overheard Nugget speaking on the microphone to someone in the game room. He told them he was going to block them, and then about a minute later, I heard him say firmly, “I don’t like the way you are talking to me, so I am going to block you now. Goodbye!" I was so proud of my son for standing up for himself and easily removing the person who was bothering him. It’s interesting how what might seem like a small issue to an adult can feel like a mountain-sized problem to a child. At the tender age of ten, Nugget was mild-mannered, warm, and loving. Apart from a few friends at school and those from our neighbourhood, he had never been exposed to individuals who intentionally tried to disturb or bully others. He was beginning to understand that there were all kinds of people in the world, and he was learning how to deal with them, one issue at a time.

Tams, on the other hand, was practically addicted to Pokémon. She collected various character plushies and often drew different Pokémon characters, even creating original creatures she thought looked “cute and cuddly.” Mr. Bonafide and I frequently bought her sketchbooks and artist pads, but within a few days, the books would be filled. When that happened, Tams would constantly ask me for plain printer paper. I soon realized that she was using up my stock so quickly that when I needed to print something, there was no paper available. While helping to organize her artwork, I discovered that Tams had over six crates filled with paper, none of which she wanted to throw away. Something had to be done, and Mr. Bonafide found the perfect solution: an artist's drawing tablet that connected to the computer. Now, all of Tams’ work could be saved digitally, eliminating the need for so much paper. Once, all the work on Tams’ computer was accidentally erased, and she fell into a deep state of despair. We all felt sorry for her when she cried for days and sulked for weeks over the loss of what had been hours and hours of her best work. Mr. Bonafide bought Tams a hard drive to use as a backup. I was relieved when I came home one evening from work and saw that Tams had returned to her artist tablet and started working on her drawings again, making sure to back up her work on the hard drive each time.

Having a teaching job brought additional supplemental income into the household, allowing Mr. Bonafide and me to feel comfortable enough to begin investing in family vacations and intimate weekend getaways for just the two of us. We strategically planned around the general school schedule and public holidays well in advance when Mr. Bonafide could request time off. Even if it was just once or twice a year, it was such a blessing for us to create the memories we made. Prior to that, we had spent over ten years living off one salary as a family of four, which required tight budgeting. I was always mindful of costs and usually refrained from taking elaborate trips. Although I longed for vacations, I never wanted us to face financial hardship because of them.

Sometimes, the desires of your heart and the dreams you create in your mind, can conflict with what your body can endure. As a seventh-grade teacher with a roster of over 140 students, I began to suffer from various stress-related illnesses that, at times, landed me in the hospital for emergency care. I was diagnosed with severe migraine headaches and later told by medical specialists that I had fibromyalgia, extreme fatigue, and irritable bowel syndrome (IBS) with constipation. My doctor advised me to change my work environment, reduce my workload, and start receiving massages and hydrotherapy to help alleviate my body's stress reactions. Wanting to feel better, I decided to leave the district at the end of the school year and use the summertime to recuperate and reconsider my options. I planned on completing substitute training to work as a substitute teacher in the Mansfield ISD.

My friend Amy informed me of a job opening for a kindergarten teacher at the elementary school where she worked. With a student load of just twenty children, I jumped at the opportunity and focused on acquiring employment with Waxahachie ISD. Working with little children thrilled me because it allowed me to be whimsical and creative. I marvelled at the beautifully stocked and well-organized kindergarten classrooms staffed by seasoned teachers from whom I could learn. During this time, I was blessed to have Mrs. Morgan in my life, a retired kindergarten teacher who had taught for about 30 years. She was assigned to my classroom during the first few weeks of my employment to monitor me and provide feedback to the administration regarding my performance and capabilities as a kindergarten teacher. Mrs. Morgan recognized my passion and experience as a teacher during her brief observations of me. Our spirits seemed to connect, and she was a woman of faith. We spent a significant amount of time discussing God's goodness. By the end of the two-week observation period, Mrs. Morgan volunteered to assist me daily in my classroom. I gained so much from her and the kindergarten team, and I was truly blessed to have supportive parents who actively participated in school events and excursions. All of these factors made my role as a kindergarten teacher more manageable. However, I was still affected by illnesses requiring me to adjust my workload further.

I constantly worried and asked myself, "Would I still be able to teach and make the impact that God wanted me to?" These thoughts weighed heavily on my mind as I came to terms with the possibility of not being able to work in a school district due to my body's reaction to stress. After just one year, I ultimately decided to leave the Waxahachie school district, and slipped into a mild depression. During this challenging time, Mr. Bonafide was a pillar of support. He reassured me that I could take my time and choose my next steps. His main desire was for me to rest, relax, and minimize my stress.

TEN

What do you do when you're forced to make a complete change in your daily operations? I considered becoming a substitute teacher, but deep down, I felt a pull toward entrepreneurship. I envisioned myself as a business owner, one who could set my own hours and work with a smaller number of children, making them easier to manage. This way, I could design my schedule and activities, and the start-up costs would be minimal.

With my creative ideas flowing, I devised a plan and shared it with Mr. Bonafide, Jew-Jew, Amy, and Mrs. Morgan to gather feedback about opening my own home-based kindergarten preparatory service and after-school tutoring program. Mr. Bonafide expressed concerns about how this change might impact our family and home dynamics. However, I convinced him it would improve my overall health and allow me to work from home.

With my plan in place, I submitted my application to establish a Limited Liability Company (LLC) with the Texas Secretary of State, obtained the necessary city permits, opened a business checking account, and launched my first official home-based tutoring business, First Start Tutoring LLC. I and my team of high school and college assistants worked with children ranging from Pre-K to 6th grade.

I began in July 2018 with a single child, a little 3-year-old girl named E.G.O. By the end of September, I had a full house with four Pre-K children during the day from 8 a.m. to 12 p.m. I also tutored a second group of four homeschooled students from 1 p.m. to 4 p.m. Additionally, I conducted three one-hour after-school tutoring sessions from 4 p.m. to 7 p.m., servicing four students per group.

Working long hours did not bother me because I had frequently worked longer as a teacher in the district. In my previous role, I often left for work as early as 7:30 a.m. and typically didn't return home until around 6 p.m. due to after-school tutoring, staff meetings, district training, or organizing my classroom for the next day's activities. Most nights, I didn't finish grading papers, entering data, or completing other work-related tasks until after 11 p.m. Working from home with my business freed me from much of that commuting and opened up a world of new possibilities, allowing me to operate as I saw fit.

As Nugget and Tams approached middle and high school, Mom suggested that I send the children to her back home for a visit. She reasoned they were old enough to travel with airline supervision, and thought it would give me a much needed break. I explained that I didn't need a break from my children; they weren't stressing me out. Additionally, I expressed doubts about sending them to Provo due to our conflicting schedules. While those reasons were genuine, there was an underlying reason for my hesitance. I still carried deep unresolved feelings of hurt from the traumas I experienced throughout the first twenty years of my life, and I did not trust my parents to fully prevent certain individuals from visiting their home. Certain individuals whom I did not trust, and with whom I felt uncomfortable. I was still secretly coping with triggers that stemmed from such conversations. I understood that the decision was mine alone regarding whether my children would visit Turks and Caicos without me, but I couldn't muster the courage to let them go. I feared that allowing them to travel without my supervision might expose them to unwanted interactions or harm. If anything were to happen, I would never forgive myself for letting them out of my sight.

Despite my attempts to explain my position to my sisters Lou, Rokie, Paulie, and Cass, I was met with reasoning and reassurances that nothing would happen to them. Some even called me selfish. I didn't care what they labelled me as; I refused to send my children to stay with anyone while they were still minors. I believed that if they wanted to travel and connect with family when they became adults, they would be able to do so. By then, I trusted that they would be competent enough to speak up for themselves.

As a mother, I felt a strong need to establish secure boundaries between my children and the outside world. My perspective was clouded by memories of extreme pain and disappointment, and I ultimately felt that I was acting in the best interests of both myself and my children. This strong will to keep my children protected led Mr. Bonafide and me to consider homeschooling them once again. It made perfect sense, as school safety was becoming a growing concern due to increased gun violence, bullying, and suicide incidents. After researching our options, Mr. Bonafide and I settled on having the children enroll in the online accredited Acellus Academy program. Taking control of our children's education was the best decision we had ever made. If we ensured that Nugget and Tams completed their academics and helped to maintain their social connections with their friends, everything would be fine.

With six courses per grade level to complete each academic semester, Nugget and Tams were on an accelerated path with the Acellus Academy to earn their high school diplomas. Instead of taking four years to finish high school, Nugget was now projected to complete everything in less than two years. Tams enrolled in the Acellus program when she was entering the seventh grade. She was projected to complete high school in only three years. Only focusing on three courses at any given time, the number of hours typically spent in regular school was drastically reduced from 7 hours to 3 or 4 hours at most.

The Acellus Academy was truly a game-changer for my tutoring business which would now be able to offer alternative options for clients who needed a different educational pathway for their children. I was experiencing a high level of satisfaction with the Acellus program, so much so, that a few of my friends and tutoring clients expressed interest in having their children unenrolled from their current schools and enrolled in the Acellus program.

My company was contracted to assist with academic coaching, tutoring, and general monitoring of daily work and progress. With the help of Zoom virtual services, I was able to incorporate the use of Acellus with my tutoring business and offer it as the primary accredited option for those clients wanting to home-school their children. Even better, I was able to comfortably cater to students from all grade levels pre-K through 12th Grade. With business booming, I soon sought the assistance of my brother P.J. to work as an online tutor, focusing on assisting students who struggled with high school math and science courses while I monitored, assisted, and tutored the students enrolled in elementary and middle school grade levels.

Personally, Acellus was also a blessing for me and my family. Gone were the issues of having to get a doctor's note for Nugget when he needed to stay home from school due to needing treatment for his asthma. When Nugget was a toddler, he was diagnosed with asthma and seasonal allergies. Nasal congestion, wheezing, and sometimes hives would flare. For the treatment of asthma, Nugget was prescribed an inhaler to use and would have to receive Albuterol breathing treatments throughout the day. At times like these, there was no need for a doctor's appointment because we knew what needed to be done; however, I would have to take Nugget to the doctor's office every time he was ill. When we switched programs, the issue of needing doctors' notes for absences was eliminated, and Nugget would be able to comfortably receive his treatment, rest, and recuperate.

By the time the COVID-19 virus reared its ugly head across America and the rest of the world, I was relieved that little to no impact was made on our personal lives since both I and the children were working and attending school at home. I became increasingly concerned, however, for my mom and my Aunty Gova, who were both battling cancer at the same time. Recently diagnosed with breast cancer, Mom stood as a formidable force in the battle of her life. She kept the word of God in her conversations and professed her faith that she was going to beat the dreaded disease that had already stripped her of her mother and two of her siblings. Not wanting my siblings and me to worry, Mom kept reassuring us that she was going to be all right. I admired the strength my mom displayed during that difficult time, and I felt terrible that I couldn't be by her side while she underwent surgeries and treatments. Meanwhile, my scoliosis was worsening, and I, too, was receiving medical care, which required a total of four surgeries within a year. All I could do to support my mom during that time was call her daily and send money to help with some of the costs.

Mom bravely faced the changes happening to her body and shared with us the moments her hair began to fall out and the moment she decided to shave it all off. She was truly beautiful, even without her hair. Her radiant smile and the genuine sparkle in her eyes were enough to capture anyone's attention. Honestly, Mom had features that suited her bald look. She reminded me of Demi Moore in the movie 'G.I. Jane,' or Sinead O'Connor with her short hair in the 'Nothing Compares 2 U' music video.

Everyone was relieved when both Aunty Gova and Mom completed their cancer treatments, and we all hoped—and kept our fingers crossed—that they would remain cancer-free. However, darkness fell over the family when Aunty Gova's cancer returned, and sadly, she was unable to endure the battle. Suddenly, what was once Tana and her four girls was reduced to just my mom. I had suffered the loss of Tana, Pinky, Babby, and Gova, leaving only Mom standing.

I began to reflect on how isolated and lonely Mom must have felt, having to navigate the loss of all her immediate family members. With only her husband and children left, she must have experienced a strong desire to cling to whatever she had left. I wanted to ensure that Mom knew how much I loved her and that I would always be there for her.

As the years went by with the business, Nugget and Tams progressed through various grade levels. Before I knew it, Nugget graduated from the Acellus Academy and earned his high school diploma. I was overjoyed and encouraged him to consider attending Tarrant County College (TCC), the local community college in our area. When Nugget shared his acceptance letter from TCC, I felt a deep sense of pride and joy. Looking at my son, I felt reassured that Mr. Bonafide and I had made the right decision to homeschool Nugget through high school. We had successfully collaborated to see him complete high school in February, and just six months later, he was stepping onto the college campus in August. I couldn't hold back the tears of pride, hope, and joy as I watched Nugget walk away from the car toward the entrance of the campus, disappearing into a sea of students.

Exactly one year later, in February, we received the high school completion letter from Acellus Academy for Tams. I looked at my beautiful daughter with love and pride. Following the steps we took when Nugget graduated, Tams applied and was accepted to TCC for the upcoming fall semester. A look of nervousness filled her eyes as if she were realizing that she was no longer a child; she had turned into a young woman. At that moment, I felt deeply that I was witnessing the closing of a chapter in my life—a chapter where I was no longer the mother of young children. I was now becoming the mother of young adults. At 44 years old, I felt satisfied with the job I had done in raising my children, knowing that I had given them my best to keep them safe, loved, and protected.

www.ingramcontent.com/pod-product-compliance
Lightning Source LLC
LaVergne TN
LVHW050338160826
845677LV00014B/3680

* 9 7 9 8 8 9 5 6 9 7 9 5 5 *